DATE DUE			

B
AIKMAN

3 3721 00282607 3
Macnow, Glen.

Sports great Troy
Aikman

D1473014

SPORTS GREAT
TROY
AIKMAN

—Sports Great Books—

BASEBALL

Sports Great Jim Abbott
0-89490-395-0/ Savage

Sports Great Bobby Bonilla
0-89490-417-5/ Knapp

Sports Great Orel Hershiser
0-89490-389-6/ Knapp

Sports Great Bo Jackson
0-89490-281-4/ Knapp

Sports Great Greg Maddux
0-89490-873-1/ Thornley

Sports Great Kirby Puckett
0-89490-392-6/ Aaseng

Sports Great Cal Ripken, Jr.
0-89490-387-X/ Macnow

Sports Great Nolan Ryan
0-89490-394-2/ Lace

Sports Great Darryl Strawberry
0-89490-291-1/ Torres & Sullivan

BASKETBALL

**Sports Great Charles Barkley
(Revised)**
0-7660-1004-X/ Macnow

Sports Great Larry Bird
0-89490-368-3/ Kavanagh

Sports Great Muggsy Bogues
0-89490-876-6/ Rekela

Sports Great Patrick Ewing
0-89490-369-1/ Kavanagh

Sports Great Anfernee Hardaway
0-89490-758-1/ Rekela

Sports Great Juwan Howard
0-7660-1065-1/ Savage

**Sports Great Magic Johnson
(Revised and Expanded)**
0-89490-348-9/ Haskins

**Sports Great Michael Jordan
(Revised)**
0-89490-978-9/ Aaseng

Sports Great Jason Kidd
0-7660-1001-5/ Torres

Sports Great Karl Malone
0-89490-599-6/ Savage

Sports Great Reggie Miller
0-89490-874-X/ Thornley

Sports Great Alonzo Mourning
0-89490-875-8/ Fortunato

Sports Great Hakeem Olajuwon
0-89490-372-1/ Knapp

**Sports Great Shaquille ONeal
(Revised)**
0-7660-1003-1/ Sullivan

Sports Great Scottie Pippen
0-89490-755-7/ Bjarkman

Sports Great Mitch Richmond
0-7660-1070-8/ Grody

**Sports Great David Robinson
(Revised)**
0-7660-1077-5/ Aaseng

Sports Great Dennis Rodman
0-89490-759-X/ Thornley

Sports Great John Stockton
0-89490-598-8/ Aaseng

Sports Great Isiah Thomas
0-89490-374-8/ Knapp

Sports Great Chris Webber
0-7660-1069-4/ Macnow

Sports Great Dominique Wilkins
0-89490-754-9/ Bjarkman

FOOTBALL

Sports Great Troy Aikman
0-89490-593-7/ Macnow

Sports Great Jerome Bettis
0-89490-872-3/ Majewski

Sports Great John Elway
0-89490-282-2/ Fox

Sports Great Brett Favre
0-7660-1000-7/ Savage

Sports Great Jim Kelly
0-89490-670-4/ Harrington

Sports Great Joe Montana
0-89490-371-3/ Kavanagh

Sports Great Jerry Rice
0-89490-419-1/ Dickey

**Sports Great Barry Sanders
(Revised)**
0-7660-1067-8/ Knapp

Sports Great Deion Sanders
0-7660-1068-6/ Macnow

Sports Great Emmitt Smith
0-7660-1002-3/ Grabowski

Sports Great Herschel Walker
0-89490-207-5/ Benagh

OTHER

Sports Great Michael Chang
0-7660-1223-9/ Ditchfield

Sports Great Oscar De La Hoya
0-7660-1066-X/ Torres

Sports Great Wayne Gretzky
0-89490-757-3/ Rappoport

Sports Great Mario Lemieux
0-89490-596-1/ Knapp

Sports Great Eric Lindros
0-89490-871-5/ Rappoport

Sports Great Steffi Graf
0-89490-597-X/ Knapp

Sports Great Pete Sampras
0-89490-756-5/ Sherrow

SPORTS GREAT
TROY
AIKMAN

Glen Macnow

— Sports Great Books—

Enslow Publishers, Inc.

40 Industrial Road   PO Box 38
Box 398   Aldershot
Berkeley Heights, NJ   07922   Hants GU12 6BP
USA   UK

http://www.enslow.com

*Dedicated to Andrew Stone, the Dallas Cowboys' No. 1 fan
and a future Hall of Famer.*

Copyright © 1995 by Glen Macnow

Library of Congress Cataloging-in-Publication Data

Macnow, Glen.
    Sports great Troy Aikman / Glen Macnow.
        p.   cm. — (Sports great books)
    Includes index.
    ISBN 0-89490-593-7
    1. Aikman, Troy, 1966- —Juvenile literature. 2. Football
    players—United States—Biography—Juvenile literature.
    [1. Aikman, Troy, 1966- . 2. Football players.]   I. Title.
    II. Series.
GV939.A46M33 1995
796.332'092—dc20
[B]
                                                94-30537
                                                    CIP
                                                    AC
Printed in the United States of America

10 9 8 7 6 5 4

To Our Readers:
All Internet addresses in this book were active and appropriate when we went to press. Any comments or suggestion can be sent by e-mail to Comments@enslow.com or to the address on the back cover.

Photo Credits: Dallas Cowboys, pp. 8, 9; James D. Smith, pp. 11, 14, 18, 21, 27, 29, 30, 34, 37, 40, 43, 45, 48, 50, 55, 57, 59.

Cover Photo: James D. Smith

Contents

Chapter 1

Troy Aikman couldn't believe his eyes. *This is too good to be true*, thought the Dallas Cowboys' young quarterback. *This is a sure thing.*

It was the second quarter of Super Bowl XXVII on January 31, 1993. Aikman's club had a narrow 14-10 lead over the Buffalo Bills. The Cowboys had the ball deep in Bills' territory. Aikman called a play that would let running back Emmitt Smith plow through Buffalo's defensive line.

But as Aikman set to take the snap from center, he noticed that Buffalo's defenders were ignoring Michael Irvin, his favorite receiver. *Yes*, Aikman thought, *this is too good to be true. This is a sure thing.*

Thinking fast, he barked out signals to change the play. When he got the ball, Aikman faked a handoff to Smith. The Bills all went for the fake. Then Aikman dropped back a few steps. He lofted a perfect spiral to Irvin, who stood alone in the end zone. Touchdown. Dallas's slim lead suddenly became 11 points. The romp was on.

Troy Aikman is considered by many to be the "Quarterback of the '90s."

Two quarters later, the Cowboys strutted off the field with a 52-17 win and the championship trophy. The game was one of the most one-sided wins in Super Bowl history. Many players could take credit. Like Smith, who rushed for 108 yards and a touchdown. Or Irvin, who caught 6 passes and outran Buffalo's secondary for 114 yards. Or Dallas's entire defense, which forced the Bills into 8 fumbles and 4 interceptions.

The biggest hero of all was Aikman. He completed 22 of 30 passes for 273 yards and 4 touchdowns. He was inspirational in calling the plays and directing his teammates. He was everyone's choice for the Super Bowl's Most Valuable Player.

In the locker room afterward, Aikman was presented with his MVP trophy and the keys to a luxury car. Reporters gathered around, perhaps expecting him to brag. But that has never been Aikman's style.

Despite Troy's wholesome appearance, he is a tough and fearless competitor on the football field.

"I'm a little bashful receiving this because we have so many great players," Aikman said. "It really is a shame they have to pick one guy."

Well, that's football, Troy. Whether it's fair or not, the quarterback gets most of the glory when his team wins a National Football League title. However, when the team loses—as the Cowboys did during Aikman's early years—the quarterback takes most of the heat.

When the team wins, the quarterback gets the biggest applause and the shiniest trophies. So when the Cowboys won the Super Bowl in 1993—and again in 1994—Troy Aikman, a quiet, shy guy from Oklahoma, suddenly emerged as an American hero.

With his powerful body and wholesome good looks, Aikman appears to be the perfect guy to play the role. He stands 6 feet 4 inches tall and weighs 220 pounds. That's big enough to bang heads with linebackers and still live to talk about it. His pinpoint accurate arm can hit a speeding receiver on the numbers from fifty yards away. His mind is so quick at reading defenses that Cowboy teammates have nicknamed him "Computer Head."

Those are the ingredients that go into this recipe. The final product is that Aikman led his team to two Super Bowl wins by the age of twenty-seven. No other quarterback in NFL history can match that feat.

Indeed, Aikman seems so perfect at what he does that you almost expect him to have a huge ego. But that's just not him. Fans like to call Joe Montana magical with his late comebacks, to call Steve Young clever and elusive, or to rave about Jim Kelly's guts. But when people talk about Aikman, they usually just say, "Oh, nice guy." There's nothing cocky or phony about this football star.

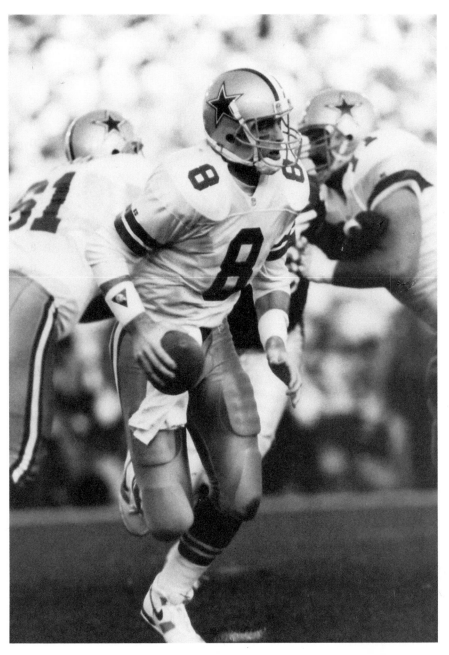

After the Dallas Cowboys' 52-17 romp over the Buffalo Bills in Super Bowl XXVII, Troy Aikman was named the game's Most Valuable Player.

"If you were to meet Troy, you'd never think he's a two-time Super Bowl star and the star quarterback for America's Team," said teammate Nate Newton. "He walks around like he's the guy who works on your car, or teaches your kids—or maybe just lives next door. He's just a regular person."

Just a regular person? Okay, maybe one with a golden arm, a quick mind, and the cool nerves of a brain surgeon. No game showed his ability to stay calm more than that first Super Bowl win over the Bills. It came before 98,374 people at the Rose Bowl in Pasadena, California.

Although he ended up as MVP of that contest, Aikman got off to a rocky start. He completed just three of his first six passes. The Cowboys punted on their first two possessions. Some fans and announcers began to wonder whether Aikman was off that day. But Troy knew things would work out. In fact, he told his teammates, "Don't worry. I feel great today. We're going to win big."

The touchdown pass to Irvin opened the gates that afternoon. But it was only one of many highlights. Aikman also threw a twenty-three-yard TD to tight end Jay Novacek, after fooling the Bills by faking another pass to Irvin. He again connected with the slippery Irvin on an eighteen-yarder in the second quarter. And he showed off his arm strength in the fourth quarter, heaving a forty-five-yard touchdown bullet to wide receiver Alvin Harper. After the game, Harper described it as the most perfect pass he had ever caught.

Two days after the Super Bowl win, the city of Dallas held a big parade for its champions. More than five hundred thousand fans gathered downtown to hear speeches by coaches and players. The one they most wanted to hear was Aikman. He was bashful in front of the big crowd and too embarrassed to talk. Teammates had to pull him to the microphone. When he finally spoke, Aikman said, "No matter what happens in my career from here on out, at least I can say that I took a team to the Super Bowl. And we were able to win it. I guess there aren't a lot of people who get the chance to say something like that."

Throughout his life, Aikman has been proving himself the best at nearly everything he has tried. Folks who remember him growing up back in Henryetta, Oklahoma, say that he could throw a strike to a teammate forty yards away at the age of twelve. In junior high, he couldn't find any receivers courageous enough to catch his bullet passes. While other fourteen-year-olds were dreaming about playing for their high school team, Aikman was doing it.

He was good enough as a teenage athlete to be offered the chance to play two sports. The New York Mets drafted him in baseball, and more than twenty colleges wanted him to play football. Young Troy finally signed on as a quarterback close to home at the University of Oklahoma. But he got injured there and ended up sitting on the bench. Eventually, he switched to UCLA. In two years, he led the Bruins to a 20-4 record. As a senior in 1988, he was a finalist for the Heisman Trophy, which goes to the best college football player in the entire country.

That same year, Dallas finished with the worst record in pro football. The terrible season got the Cowboys' coach fired. It also gave them the first choice in the 1989 draft of college seniors. When it came time to make the pick, there was little question whom Dallas would select.

"Troy has the talent to take the Cowboys back to where we all want them to be," new coach Jimmy Johnson said on draft day. "You would be amazed at what some of the teams were willing to give up in a trade for Troy. But we've known that this was our guy."

In Aikman's first year, things didn't go exactly as he or the coach had planned. The Cowboys had more than a dozen other rookies, including most of the men who blocked for the quarterback. They all suffered through growing pains. No one suffered more than Troy, who was decked so many times that he earned the nickname "Timex." That comes from the watch company's old ad slogan—"It takes a licking, but keeps on ticking."

The Cowboys won just one game that season and just seven in 1990. But by 1991, Aikman emerged as a star. The Cowboys made the playoffs that season for the first time in six years. With a young team and a young quarterback, Dallas began to earn respect around the league. Some experts, including Chicago Bears coach Mike Ditka, predicted that

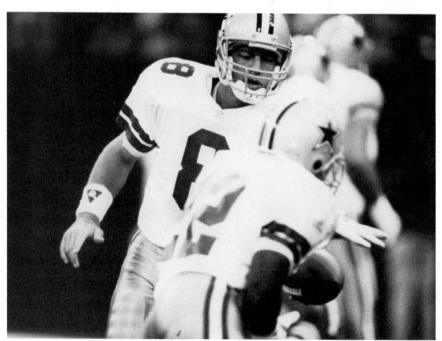

Aikman hands off the ball to running back Emmitt Smith, another superstar on the Dallas Cowboys' roster.

Aikman would lead the Cowboys to a Super Bowl in two or three more years.

Ditka was wrong. It didn't take the Cowboys two or three years to make it. It took just one. In the magical 1992 season, Dallas won 13 regular-season games and lost just three. Aikman, with good players now surrounding him, threw for 23 touchdowns. He made the NFL's all-star game, the Pro Bowl, for the first time.

His shining moment, of course, came in the Super Bowl. Afterward, Aikman would say that his favorite highlight was the first touchdown pass to Irvin, the one that broke open the game.

"When I saw how the Bills weren't covering Michael tight, I could hardly believe my eyes," he said. "It was a very special moment for me, because that's when I realized that we were going to be the champions. It was a long road. It took a lot of different courses to get to where I am now."

Chapter 2

As a young boy, Troy Aikman dreamed of becoming a major league baseball pitcher. Growing up in Cerritos, California, his heroes were players on the Los Angeles Dodgers—not the Los Angeles Rams. Young Troy's arm—a rifle even back then—made him a nine-year-old pitching star in Little League. Football? That was just a game to play on the rare days that it got too chilly for baseball.

That all changed when Troy was twelve. His father, Ken Aikman, got a good job working on an oil pipeline and moved the family to a ranch in tiny Henryetta, Oklahoma. The new neighborhood did not have shopping malls or fast-food restaurants for Troy to bike to. The closest neighbors lived nearly a mile away. Troy was so unhappy about leaving his California friends that he didn't speak to his parents for two weeks. When he finally stopped sulking and looked around his new hometown, he noticed that the kids didn't play baseball nearly as much as football.

Troy had not liked football much since he broke his wrist playing it at age ten. But he wanted to make new friends, and he wanted to please his dad who was a big fan of the sport. So the new eighth-grader went out for football. "In Oklahoma," Troy later explained, "everybody plays football whether they want to or not. It's the manly thing to do."

On the first day of practice in junior high school, the coaches asked Troy to pick a position. He chose quarterback. They handed him a ball. He threw a perfect thirty-yard spiral that stung the hands of the boy who tried to grab it. He threw more passes, but they were too fast for the other kids to catch. So the coaches quickly sent Troy to another field to work out with the older high school boys.

The high school coach, Barry Holt, immediately noticed something funny about the youngster's passing style. Instead of putting all of his fingers on the football's laces, as most quarterbacks do, Troy put only his pinkie on the laces. It was a strange delivery, but it worked for Troy. So the coach wisely decided not to change it. These days, Aikman is the only quarterback in the NFL to handle the ball in this unusual way.

By the time he was fourteen, Troy was starting for the Henryetta High Fighting Hens. The team lost more games than it won in two of Troy's three seasons there, but he became famous around Oklahoma as a strong-armed kid who might someday end up in the NFL. The players and coaches all knew Aikman was special. Local football fans in Henryetta still talk about some of his more memorable plays.

Against Hartshorne High one Friday night, Henryetta was 7 points down in the last 2 minutes. Aikman was trying to drive the Hens to the winning score. He dropped back to pass but was hit by two defensive linemen. As he was falling backward, Aikman reached out and threw a twenty-five-yard sidearm touchdown pass. After the game, Hartshorne's coach told Troy, "We'll be watching you someday on Monday Night Football."

Troy's high school coach was the first to notice his unusual passing style. Most quarterbacks put all their fingers on the football's laces, but Aikman only rests his pinkie there. Today, Troy is the only quarterback in the NFL to handle the ball in this unusual way.

Another time, the Fighting Hens were tied with Checotah High, 6-6, with 30 seconds left. Troy threw a seventy-yard touchdown pass to win the game. As his teammates danced and screamed on the sidelines, Troy calmly walked over and drank a glass of water. John Walker, who was a friend and teammate, later said that kind of calm reaction was typical. Aikman never said a lot, Walker explained. A player of his great ability didn't need to say much.

According to Aikman, that's just what he learned from his parents, Ken and Charlyn Aikman. "What I am is a direct result of how I was raised," he said. "I don't understand why guys want to be controversial and in the press all the time. It's just not my nature."

The folks in Henryetta appreciated Troy's modest and friendly ways. Indeed, they still do. The town of 7,000 now has an "Aikman Avenue" and "Home of Troy Aikman" signs on the city limits. After his Super Bowl win, Aikman donated money to help build a children's center in town. He also sponsors a scholarship for students who want to attend college but can't afford to.

That wasn't on his mind back in high school. Back then, he was still trying to make the tough choice between baseball and football. Although he was the state of Oklahoma's top high school quarterback as a senior, Troy still loved playing baseball. He had grown to six-feet-four and was Henryetta High's star catcher and shortstop. The night before major league baseball's 1984 draft of prospects, a scout from the New York Mets came to visit. The scout told Troy that club was thinking of taking him—as long as his signing-bonus request was reasonable.

It was tempting, Troy thought, but it was also wrong. He had promised his father that he would go to college and study to be a doctor. Playing football would earn him that chance to go to college. So Troy blurted out a contract demand—$200,000—that he hoped would be too high for the Mets. The scout's response: "Good luck playing football."

Dozens of college coaches lined up to get Troy. His first choice was Oklahoma State. The coach there was Jimmy Johnson, who ran a high-octane passing attack that Aikman loved. Years later, Johnson and Aikman would come together as coach and quarterback of the Dallas Cowboys. But back in 1984, Troy was talked out of going to Oklahoma State by Barry Switzer. He was the coach of the University of Oklahoma Sooners.

Switzer, a famous coach, ran the state's top football program. Every high school player in Oklahoma dreamed of playing for him. Aikman shared that dream. But he was not excited about Switzer's so-called "wishbone" offense, which used the quarterback more as a runner than a passer. Aikman had a golden arm and wanted to use it.

"No problem," Switzer said. Because Aikman was so talented, the coach told him, the school would change its offensive plan. With Aikman as quarterback, Switzer promised to drop the wishbone for a wide-open passing game.

Troy believed the promise. He signed up for the school. Later he learned that Switzer had told other people he would never change his offensive plan for anyone. "I guess I got suckered," Aikman said. "Coach Switzer talked to me about playing for the Orange Bowl and the national championship every year. I wanted to do those things."

Stuck in a bad situation, Troy decided to make the best of it. He outworked his teammates, on the field and off. He always carried a notepad, writing down every word said by every coach. When no one else knew the answer, recalled offensive coordinator Tony Brown, coaches could ask Troy.

20

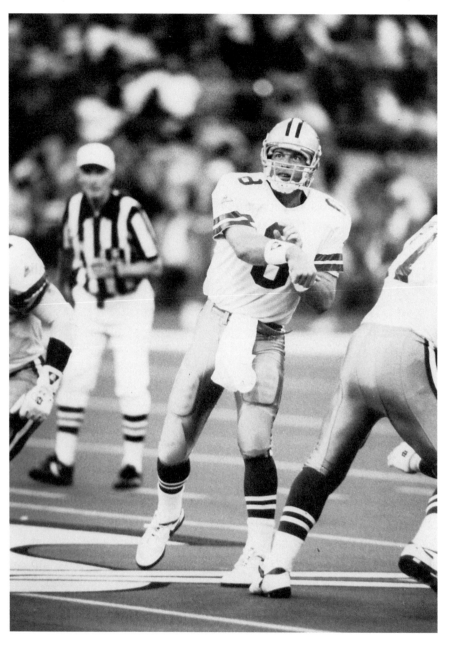

When Aikman was sidelined at the University of Oklahoma, he realized that he would have to become a star at another college to achieve his dream of playing in the NFL. He transferred to UCLA and took the Bruins to a Cotton Bowl victory.

He would always know it. Aikman was driven to be a great player.

As an eighteen-year-old freshman, Troy was forced into a starting role against Kansas when quarterback Danny Bradley was injured. As hard as he had worked, he wasn't ready. He completed just 2 of 14 pass attempts for 8 yards and 3 interceptions. The Sooners lost, 28-11. Some of the hometown fans booed Aikman.

The next season, 1985, Troy was more prepared. He started Oklahoma's first three games—all wins. Coach Switzer, impressed with Aikman's arm, was letting him throw more passes. In the fourth game, against the University of Miami, Aikman completed 6 of 7 passes for 131 yards and a touchdown in the first quarter. Oklahoma seemed ready to win the game. Then disaster struck.

Aikman dropped back to pass early in the second quarter. Miami blitzed, meaning it sent six pass rushers after the quarterback. Two of them caught Aikman, rolled over him and broke his ankle. His season was finished.

So, in fact, was his career as a Sooner. Freshman Jamelle Holieway took over the quarterback's job. He led Oklahoma to a national championship. When the next season started, Holieway had the job. Troy was back on the bench. "We will see Aikman in the NFL," coach Switzer said at the time. "We will not see Jamelle Holieway in the NFL. But Holieway fits our system better."

Aikman knew that to get to the NFL, he'd have to first be a star at another college. So he went to see Switzer. The coach offered to help by calling coaches he knew to see who might be interested in a rifle-armed quarterback coming off an ankle injury.

One of Switzer's first calls went to Terry Donahue, coach at the University of California at Los Angeles. Donahue didn't know much about Troy. Switzer promised him that Troy was better than any other quarterback UCLA had. That was good enough for Donahue. He invited Troy to become a Bruin. For Aikman, it was a second chance to become a starter—this time for a team that liked to throw the ball. And it was a chance to go back to southern California for the first time since he was a young boy.

Aikman felt as if his dreams had all come true. Now he just had to show how talented he could be.

Chapter 3

When Troy arrived on UCLA's campus in 1987, the school already had a starting quarterback. His name was Brendan McCracken. The Bruins' quarterback coach, Rick Neuheisel, expected that Aikman wouldn't know much about passing because his old school, Oklahoma, didn't throw much. The new guy figured to be a backup, nothing more. But when they met, Neuheisel found himself staring at Aikman's big, muscular frame. And when they shook hands, Aikman's hand was so big that it seemed to swallow the coach's. Neuheisel realized then that Troy would be something special.

Actually, Troy had always been special. At UCLA, Troy showed he knew how to throw a speed ball over the middle or a feathery pass just over the defenders' arms. He was always the first one to get to team meetings. He was always the last one out of the weight room because he worked so hard. And he was tough.

At first, Troy's new teammates were not ready to accept him. Many wanted their old buddy, McCracken, to keep the starter's job. But Aikman worked hard to win over the other players. And he played so well in practices that everyone—including McCracken—agreed that Troy was the best quarterback on campus.

In his first game, Aikman completed 8 of 10 passes for 166 yards. The Bruins whipped San Diego State, 47-14. A new star had arrived. For the season, Troy went on to complete 65 percent of his passes. He threw for 17 touchdowns and just 8 interceptions. UCLA won 10 of its 12 games, including a victory over Nebraska in the Aloha Bowl.

That great season made Troy into a national celebrity. Suddenly, he was regarded as one of the nation's top college football stars. Indeed, before his senior year, many sportswriters predicted Aikman would win the Heisman Trophy.

Some young players might let that kind of attention go to their heads, but not Aikman. He's still a down-to-earth guy. In fact, he spent the summer before his senior year working as a construction worker. No late-night Hollywood parties for Troy. Instead, he worked hard all day, studied his play books at night, and went to bed early.

His hard work and dedication paid off. In 1989, Troy picked up where he left off. He led the Bruins to another 10-2 season and another post-season victory, this time in the Cotton Bowl. As a senior, he passed for 2,771 yards and 24 touchdowns and threw only 9 interceptions. His final statistics made him the third-highest rated passer in collegiate history.

Aikman's final college game was one of his best. On January 2, 1989, he led UCLA on two long touchdown drives to beat Arkansas, 17-3, in the Cotton Bowl. It was a special win for the Bruins because it was their seventh straight bowl victory. That set an NCAA record.

The win didn't come easily. Playing before 74,000 fans—including 150 of his friends and relatives—Troy threw an interception on his third pass. But he quickly recovered and led UCLA on scoring drives of 93 and 74 yards. The second touchdown drive was especially impressive. With just two minutes left in the first half, the Bruins got the ball at their own twenty-four-yard line. Troy tried to beat the clock by throwing six straight passes. He completed each one. With just seconds to go in the half, he had a third-and-goal on Arkansas' one-yard line. Troy wrapped the ball under his arm and ran to his right. He was faking a bootleg play. When Arkansas' defenders began to chase him, Aikman flipped a touchdown pass over the line to tight end Corwin Anthony.

After the game, Arkansas safety Steve Atwater was asked his thoughts on Aikman. "He's the $1-million man," said Atwater. "He's very agile and hard to contain on the rollout. He's got great zip on the ball." Atwater said that in his four years of college, Aikman was the best player he had played against.

Was he the best college player in the country? That depends how you look at it. Troy did not win the Heisman Trophy that year. That honor went to Barry Sanders, the Oklahoma State running back. Sanders led all college players in rushing. He, too, would become an NFL superstar.

Most experts, however, agreed that Troy was the college player who would make the biggest splash in pro football. In fact, many people called him the best quarterback prospect since John Elway left college in 1983. So when the NFL draft rolled around in April 1989, there was no doubt that the first pick—the biggest prize—would be the tall, strong kid from Henryetta, Oklahoma.

The NFL draft allows the team with the worst record to pick the best young player. The Dallas Cowboys had been to the playoffs five times in the 1980s. But by 1988 they had the worst record in the league. The Cowboys had not had a

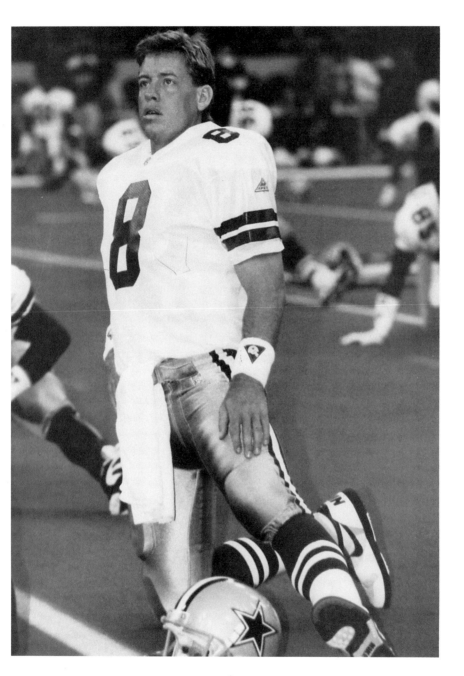

As a student player, Troy was always the first on the field and the last in the weight room. He took his good work habits with him to the NFL. Here he warms up before a game against Minnesota.

winning quarterback since Roger Staubach retired ten years earlier. As it turns out, Staubach was Aikman's favorite player as a child.

"You've got to have a good quarterback," said Cowboys president Tex Schramm. "It is, it has been, and it always will be the name of the game. The quarterback has got to win some football games for you. You can squeeze by here and there, but the quarterback will always be the heart of your club."

The lowly Cowboys liked everything they saw in Aikman. Team vice president Gil Brandt went to scout him and came back praising Troy's size, arm, athletic ability, work habits, character, toughness, and intelligence.

The club dropped a few hints that it would consider trading the top draft pick. No one really believed it. Aikman seemed too perfect a fit for Dallas.

And that was fine with Troy. The Cowboys had been his favorite team since he moved to Oklahoma as a boy. He liked their field at Texas Stadium. He liked their uniforms, with the shiny blue star on the helmet. He liked their coach, Tom Landry.

Make that, he liked their former coach. On February 25, 1989, Arkansas millionaire Jerry Jones bought the Dallas Cowboys. Jones's first move was to fire Coach Landry and hire a new head coach, Jimmy Johnson. Aikman and Johnson had an interesting history. When Johnson was the head coach at Oklahoma State in 1984, he almost convinced Troy to play there. In 1985, when Troy was at Oklahoma, Johnson became the head coach at the University of Miami. It was against Johnson's team that Aikman had broken his ankle, which knocked him out for the season. Then, when Troy transferred from Oklahoma, Johnson tried without luck to lure him to Miami.

So this was Johnson's third chance to get Troy. He didn't waste any time. Even before the draft, the Cowboys and Aikman began working on a deal. They got it wrapped up the day before the draft. Aikman received a six-year, $11 million contract. It was the most money ever promised to a first-year player. Aikman was presented with a new No. 8 Cowboys jersey. He then was led to his new locker and introduced to his new teammates. The next day he flew to New York City to meet NFL Commissioner Pete Rozelle and face reporters.

"I have dreamed about being in this spot all of my life," Aikman told the reporters. "I set some pretty high goals at an early age and I'm not going to let anything stand in my way.

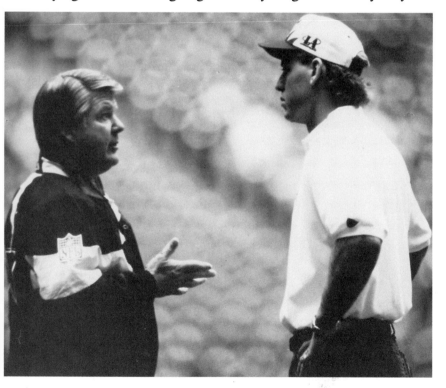

Jimmy Johnson was hired as head coach right before Troy was drafted by the Dallas Cowboys.

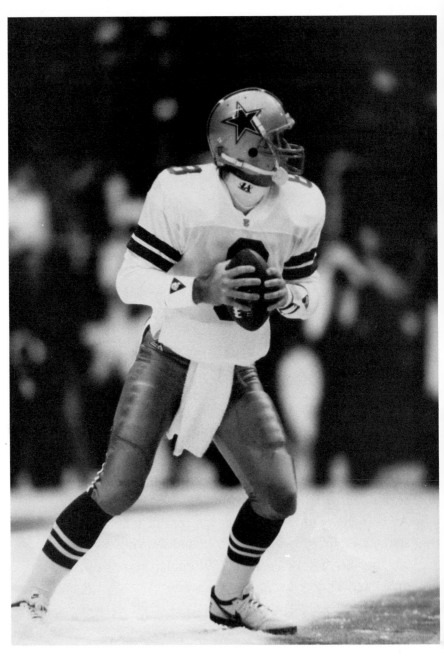

To gain the starting quarterback position on the team, Troy worked extra hard and let his arm do the talking.

When I was growing up, I watched Roger Staubach on TV quite a bit. Every time we turned on the TV, the Cowboys were on. It seems like they never lost a game. They could be down three touchdowns with a minute to play and they'd win. I guess people have had a hard time trying to fill his shoes. I'll try to do my best."

It was modest talk, the kind he had learned from his dad. Ken Aikman had always told his son to lead by actions, not by words. So one of Troy's first actions after signing was to establish yearly $5,000 scholarships at both Henryetta High and UCLA. He also promised to donate $1,000 to charity for each game won by the Cowboys.

Nice as he was, there were still some questions about how older Cowboys might react to this rookie. Troy's salary made him the club's best-paid player before he had even walked onto an NFL field. So it would be natural for some veterans to be jealous. And, just like when Aikman moved to UCLA, there was a popular starting quarterback already in place in Dallas. Steve Pelluer hadn't won many games for the Cowboys, but he had won a lot of friends.

Troy kept quiet and decided to let his arm do the talking. Even when the Cowboys used a special first-round pick that summer to draft another college quarterback, Steve Walsh, Aikman did not complain. He was confident he could win the starter's job by working extra hard and showing his talent.

And he did. When the 1989 regular season opened, top draft pick Troy Aikman was the starter. The Cowboys had a new quarterback, a new coach and twenty new players. The fans in Dallas were excited. It was a new era for the team. Maybe, fans figured, the Cowboys would return to the form that put them in five Super Bowls in the 1970s. Maybe, Aikman would be the man to lead them there.

Troy certainly hoped so. He entered his rookie season full of confidence. Would the Cowboys have a winning record? Would they make the playoffs? Troy believed that they might.

He would soon find out that the NFL was tougher than he had expected.

Chapter 4

Troy Aikman knew that pro football would be tough. He did not expect to come straight from UCLA and dominate the NFL. The pro players were bigger, faster, more experienced than those he faced in college. His rookie season would be one for learning, he figured.

Troy's first year was twice as tough as he had expected. When a rookie quarterback plays for a losing team, he must quickly learn how to take shots from opposing players. The 1989 Cowboys were a team of inexperienced young players and over-the-hill older players. As a result, Aikman got little blocking and spent much of that year flat on his back, staring up at the opponents who decked him.

Actually, things started out well. The Cowboys opened with four preseason games. Those are practice games that don't count in the standings. Dallas won three of the four games. Aikman looked terrific. In his first preseason game, against the San Diego Chargers, Troy completed 8 of 11 passes. He threw a nine-yard touchdown pass to Kelvin Martin. And he launched a fifty-one-yard bomb to second-year receiver Michael Irvin. After the game, Irvin said he had been wondering if Troy had a strong enough arm to throw such a long pass. Now he knew. "He can throw as deep as I can run," Irvin said. "I think he's going to have a great season."

Not exactly. Once the real season began, opposing teams took things more seriously. The Cowboys had a handful of good players, including Irvin and running back Herschel Walker, but new coach Jimmy Johnson had gotten rid of most of the older players. He replaced them with inexperienced rookies. The new players showed some promise. But they were not ready to face the likes of the Eagles, Giants, Redskins, and 49ers.

Surrounded by other rookie players, Troy was frequently sacked in his early days with the Cowboys. A fearless competitor, Troy would always head back into the game after a beating from the opponents.

Aikman started the first game of his rookie year. Dallas was shut out by the New Orleans Saints. For the season, the Cowboys went 1-15. Troy didn't play in that one win. He broke his index finger against the New York Giants and had to sit out a month. The Cowboys lost all twelve games in which he played. The team's only win came with the other rookie quarterback, Steve Walsh, running the show.

Still, there was reason to feel good about Aikman. Troy was fearless. When he took a beating, he went back into the game, instead of back to the bench. He showed poise. That means he didn't get rattled when faced with new, confusing situations. And he kept his spirits up and tried to rally his teammates to play better. "We may not get to the Super Bowl this season," Aikman told the others. "But if we stick together, we should get there some day."

One man who shared that opinion was Washington Redskins coach Joe Gibbs. After beating the Cowboys by a 30-7 score early that season, Gibbs met with reporters in the locker room. Everyone expected him to praise his own club, but Gibbs's kindest words went to the losing team's quarterback. "From what I've seen," Gibbs said. "Aikman is very talented, gifted, and tough. He's going to be very bad for the Redskins and the rest of the teams in this division."

Troy's best game as a rookie came against the Phoenix Cardinals. It was his first game back after the finger injury. Aikman set the NFL single-game, rookie record when he threw for 379 yards. That mark still stands, but Troy will remember the game more for one single play. The play—an 80-yard touchdown pass—showed everything that was right with Aikman and wrong with the Cowboys in 1989.

It came late in the fourth quarter with the Cowboys trailing, 17-13. Troy faded back to pass, scrambling to gain more time. From the corner of his eye, he spotted wide receiver James Dixon streaking for the end zone. Troy heaved the ball as far as he could.

At exactly that moment, Aikman was blasted from behind by Cardinals linebacker Anthony Bell. He did a cartwheel before crashing to the ground. He lay there motionless. Blood flowed from his right ear onto the blue star of his helmet. As team doctors began to examine Troy, several coaches on the sideline feared that he had been killed.

He hadn't. But he did suffer a hit to the head that knocked him out for more than five minutes. Despite that, his pass sailed into Dixon's outstretched hands. The touchdown gave Dallas a 20-17 lead with less than two minutes to play.

When Troy finally came to, he didn't believe he had thrown for a touchdown, until he noticed the changed numbers on the scoreboard. But seconds later, the Cardinals came back to score and win the game, 24-20. Aikman could hardly believe that either.

Despite flashes of brilliance by the rookie quarterback, the Cowboys still couldn't win. They had such a long way to go.

Afterward, Aikman sat on a stool in front of his locker and spoke of his disappointment. "It has been a long season so far," he said. "I don't know how a rookie is supposed to feel. I'm not going to sit here and tell you I feel like a seasoned veteran and know everything teams are trying to do. Because that's not the truth. But I feel good out there for the most part. And I don't want anyone around me to sense that I'm a rookie. I don't want to be a problem."

Troy was hardly a problem for the Cowboys. When the season ended, he had passed for 1,749 yards. That was a record for Dallas rookies. He was chosen for most all rookie teams. He threw 9 touchdowns, which was good. And he threw 18 interceptions, which was bad. Overall, he showed signs that he could be an excellent NFL quarterback. Coach

When Troy's first season ended, he had broken the Dallas rookie record for passing and was chosen for most all-rookie teams.

Johnson said Aikman had the physical and mental talent to lead the Cowboys through the 1990s.

Now, all Johnson had to do was build a solid team around Troy. Actually, the coach started building even during the 1989 season. He traded star running back Herschel Walker for a package of five players and seven draft picks. Then, in 1990, the Cowboys drafted running back Emmitt Smith. Almost immediately, Smith became a superstar. And Smith's great running forced other teams to stop focusing only on Aikman. Through trades and drafts, Johnson kept adding good, young players. And he subtracted one—quarterback Steve Walsh, whom he traded to the Saints.

When Walsh was around, Aikman seemed to be always looking over his shoulder, wondering if Walsh would steal his job. Now Aikman knew he was the only quarterback in the Cowboys' future. His teammates knew it too.

By the time Troy started his second season, he felt much better. The Cowboys might not get to the Super Bowl, he figured, but they would win their share of games.

They did. Starting with the season opener against the San Diego Chargers, Aikman got the ball with two minutes to go and the Cowboys behind by 4 points. He quickly moved the team fifty-three yards. A twenty-four-yard touchdown pass to Kelvin Martin brought Dallas the win—the first of Aikman's career. Afterward, Troy said he felt as if a giant weight had been lifted from his back. "I don't have to listen to people say I can't win a ball game anymore," he said. "People were questioning the kind of team we were going to have. We worked too hard not to become a good football team."

The Cowboys continued to struggle toward their goal. They won seven games in 1990—six more than the year before. But they still lost nine. Emmitt Smith rushed for more than 900 yards and was named the NFL's Rookie of the Year.

Other young players kept getting better. But the Cowboys still made too many mistakes.

They had much to learn.

Mostly, they needed to learn to better protect the quarterback. Aikman was sacked (tackled for a loss) thirty-nine times that season. At least twice that often, he was hit hard right after passing the ball. He got decked so often that his nickname around the NFL became "Troy Ache-Man." After every game, it seemed, another part of his body was being X-rayed.

The worst day came in the second-to-last game of the season. The Cowboys were 7-7 at the time. If they could somehow beat the tough Philadelphia Eagles, they still had some hope of making the playoffs. But on the game's fifth play, Aikman was sacked from behind by Eagles defensive end Clyde Simmons. The 300-pound Simmons drove Aikman's right shoulder into the turf and then rolled over it.

Troy was badly hurt. His shoulder was separated. He was out for the game, which the Cowboys lost, 17-3. And he missed the final game of the season, which they also lost. As soon as the season ended, Troy had two operations. His shoulder was popped back into place. Bone chips were removed from his right elbow. Doctors told him he would be as good as new. They also told him he had been taking too many hits. If he wanted to keep playing football, he would have to get better protection from his teammates.

The last message, actually, went straight to Jimmy Johnson. The Cowboys coach listened. In his mind, the team was on the verge of becoming great. All that was needed was a strong offensive line. So Johnson built that line. Through trades, draft picks, and free agent moves he assembled a crew

In a game against the Philadelphia Eagles, a 300-pound defensive end landed on Troy's shoulder and separated it. Doctors told Coach Johnson that Troy would have to be better protected on the field if he wanted to keep playing football.

of giants: center Mark Stepnoski, guards John Gesek and Nate Newton, and tackles Erik Williams and Kevin Gogan. The five men averaged 6 feet 5 inches and 301 pounds. Their size and strength would keep would-be tacklers away in 1992, Johnson figured.

The coach was right. And the Cowboys—led by a well-protected Aikman—would finally become winners.

Chapter 5

Before the 1991 season, Aikman spent a month back home in Oklahoma. He wanted to escape from the pressures in Dallas. He wanted to clear his head. So he returned to Henryetta—driving a new car he bought as a surprise for his mom. He visited his older sisters, Tammy and Terri. He spent hours playing with his nieces and nephews. He even hung around his old high school pals, playing relaxed games of catch.

In his own way, Troy was preparing for a new season. He wanted to do it his way. He wanted to remember what had made him so successful in high school and college. He wanted to find that formula and bring it to the Cowboys. He was tired of losing.

After a month, Troy found what he was looking for. The solution seemed too simple. "I've got to start being myself," he told friends. "I've got to stop trying to become the quarterback that others want me to be, and start doing what I do best."

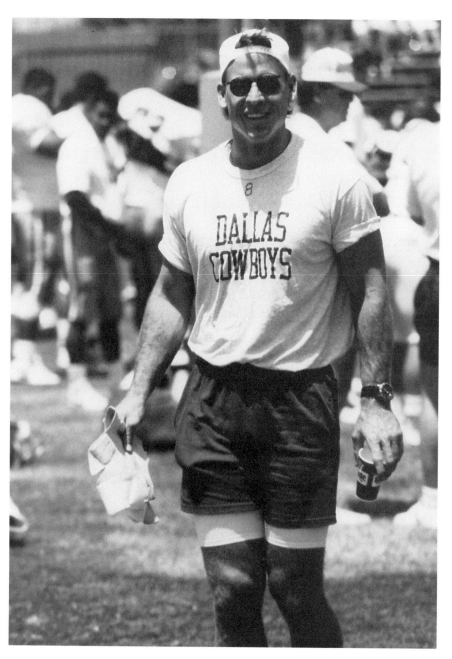

Troy still works on his game during the off-season. Here, he takes a quick break at the team's training camp in Austin, Texas.

That meant playing in his own style, passing the ball with his special quick release. It meant acting more like himself, instead of what he felt others wanted him to be. It meant having more confidence in his own decisions.

Aikman flew back to Dallas and shared his ideas with coach Jimmy Johnson. Surprisingly, Johnson liked it. Following Troy's ideas, the Cowboys began a quick-release offense, designed to keep the quarterback in one piece. And Johnson told Troy to take more control of the club. "Change the plays at the line of scrimmage if you like," Johnson said. "Become a team leader. It's your third year," the coach told Troy. "It's your time to become a star."

The strategy worked. In 1991, Troy grew from a battered quarterback into a leader. He threw for 2,754 yards and completed 65 percent of his passes. Both were career highs, he threw just 10 interceptions. Dallas's beefy new offensive line got a lot of the credit. So did Coach Johnson's new offense. Troy's determination and maturity played a big part. His plan to change his ways and play in the style that made him a success in high school and college had worked.

The Cowboys won 11 games in 1991 and lost just 5. They made the playoffs for the first time in six years. They even beat the Chicago Bears in the playoffs before being knocked out by the Detroit Lions. It was a great season for the club.

Sadly, Troy wasn't around for all of it. In the season's twelfth game, he was tackled hard by Washington Redskins defensive end Charles Mann. Aikman sprained his knee on the play. He missed the season's last four games and the first playoff game while backup Steve Beuerlein filled in. Troy came back to play in the playoffs against Detroit.

The season ended in a disappointing 38-6 loss to the Lions. Still, there was a lot to be excited about in Dallas. Aikman was picked to play in his first Pro Bowl, the NFL's all-star game. He and his teammates figured that 1991 was a preview of great things to come. Others agreed, including Roger Staubach, the former Cowboys star quarterback who had been Troy's hero as a youngster. After watching the 1991 season, Staubach made a bold prediction that the Cowboys would be in the next Super Bowl, and Troy Aikman would lead them there.

Staubach was right. In 1992, Troy and the Cowboys finally put it all together. The team won 13 regular-season games and lost just three. Aikman threw 23 touchdowns. He ranked third in the ratings of NFL passers. Behind a now-solid offensive line, he stayed healthy the entire season. He had emerged as the star everyone predicted he would be.

At the beginning of Troy's third season with the Cowboys, Coach Johnson encouraged him to take on the role of team leader. Here, he discusses a call with one of the back judges during a game against the Miami Dolphins.

The Cowboys had many stars in 1992. Running back Emmitt Smith led the NFL with 1,713 rushing yards and 18 touchdowns. Wide receiver Michael Irvin caught 78 passes—76 of them thrown by Aikman. In all, six players on the team were chosen for the Pro Bowl.

The key man—despite all the other stars—was Aikman. "When you prepare for the Cowboys, it begins with Aikman," said San Francisco 49ers coach George Seifert.

"It's easy to take him for granted because they're so talented that moving the ball looks easy. But he's big and strong. He's got an accurate arm. And he's got a leadership quality about him."

Seifert was about to find out how super Aikman could be. In January 1993, the 49ers and Cowboys met in the NFC title game. The winner would go to the Super Bowl. The Cowboys had not been to the Super Bowl in fourteen years. Aikman had the chance to be a hero in Dallas.

Aikman accomplished his mission. Against San Francisco, he completed 24 of 34 passes for 322 yards and 2 touchdowns. He led the Cowboys to a 30-20 victory.

His best work was in the second half. Troy directed three touchdown drives to win the game. He was nearly perfect, completing 13 of 16 passes. Mostly, Aikman did what he does best. He didn't turn the ball over. He dented the defense with short passes underneath. When the time was right, he hurt the 49ers with the long pass.

Late in the game, the 49ers scored. The Dallas lead was just 24-20, and the game seemed ready to slip away. Aikman got the ball on his own twenty-four-yard line. Some of the team's coaches wanted to play it safe and try a few running plays, but Aikman convinced head coach Jimmy Johnson to go for it all.

On first down, Troy faked a handoff to Smith. Then he faded back and lofted a perfect pass into the hands of wide receiver Alvin Harper. San Francisco's defenders were surprised. Harper ran seventy yards, all the way to the San Francisco six-yard line. Three plays later, Aikman hit wide receiver Kelvin Martin with a touchdown pass.

The game belonged to Dallas. The Cowboys were going to the Super Bowl.

"I think a lot of people didn't know Troy would be as good as he is," said wide receiver Michael Irvin. "He's a one-of-a-kind guy. He has all the confidence in the world in his ability. We believe in him too."

Irvin and his teammates had reason to believe. After three years of frustration, the guy they called "Ache-Man" had come into his own. Now he needed to have one more big game.

The Cowboys faced the Buffalo Bills in Super Bowl XXVII. While Aikman and nearly all of his young teammates had never been there before, the Bills were back for their third straight appearance. Buffalo had lost the two previous Super Bowls, to the New York Giants and the Washington Redskins. Now the Bills were hungry for a title.

Buffalo was led by quarterback Jim Kelly. Like Aikman, he was a Pro Bowl star. Otherwise, the two men couldn't be more different. Kelly is loud and friendly. He likes to go to parties and to tell jokes. Aikman, meanwhile, has always been quiet and a bit of a loner. He's not unfriendly. He just prefers a quiet, peaceful life. While Kelly's idea of a snack is nachos and beer, Aikman's has always been cookies and milk.

The two quarterbacks' playing styles are also different. Kelly is a daredevil. Sometimes he defies the odds by throwing to receivers who seem to be covered. It causes more

The Cowboys defeated the San Francisco 49ers, 30-20, in the 1993 NFC title game and won their ticket to a Super Bowl showdown against the Buffalo Bills.

interceptions. But it creates more touchdowns for his team, too.

Aikman is more careful. He'll rarely throw the ball into double-coverage. Instead, he'll stand in the pocket, searching until the last possible moment for an open receiver. The result is that he often gets sacked for a loss or nailed by a tackler.

But he throws few interceptions.

Super Bowl XXVII, on January 31, 1993, was billed as a battle between these two quarterbacks. Sure, there were other great players on both teams: runners Emmitt Smith of the Cowboys and Thurman Thomas of the Bills; receivers Michael Irvin of the Cowboys and Andre Reed of the Bills. Aikman and Kelly were the players who best represented what their teams stood for. Everyone wanted to see which quarterback would come out on top.

It wasn't even close. The Cowboys rode over the Bills, winning 52-17. Kelly tossed two interceptions and was knocked out of the game in the second quarter. Aikman, meanwhile, was brilliant. After a slow start, he passed for 272 yards and 4 touchdowns.

It all started clicking for Aikman and his speedy band of receivers on their third drive. The Bills had taken a 7-0 lead. And this drive started as poorly as Dallas's first two—Emmitt Smith lost one yard on first down. Then, Aikman's pass to Smith ended up losing another five.

On third-and-sixteen from Dallas's forty-seven, Irvin ran a square-in pattern. The Cowboys' offensive line gave Aikman time, and he fired a twenty-yard strike to Irvin that seemed to lift the entire team. Three plays later, Aikman connected over the middle with tight end Jay Novacek for a twenty-three-yard TD.

Once the TDs started coming, they kept coming. And Dallas got stronger as the game wore on. In the end, Dallas's

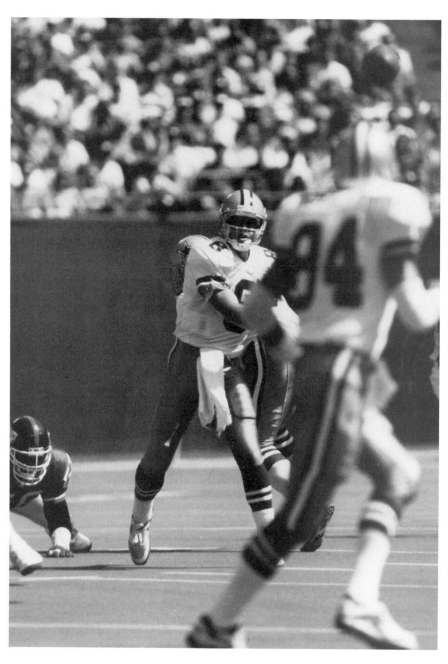

Troy's rifle-arm fires a pass to tight end Jay Novacek.

35-point win was the third-highest margin of victory in Super Bowl history.

Aikman was everyone's choice for the game's Most Valuable Player award. He did a commercial for Disney World while running off the field. In the locker room afterward, he was handed his MVP trophy.

He used the moment to remember his rookie season. The Cowboys went 1-15 that year. Troy had spent much of that season on his back, looking up. As reporters gathered around, Aikman said, "Those were tough days. At times I felt a little overwhelmed. It's hard to believe that in four seasons, we've gone from being that bad to being champions. It's a sweet feeling."

The only thing that would make it sweeter, would be another Super Bowl title.

Chapter 6

Every great quarterback has his own style. Just look at the greats of past decades.

Baltimore's Johnny Unitas, the best of the 1950s, was cool and calm. He almost never made a bad throw or a bad decision. Joe Namath, the New York Jets' star of the 1960s, was a daredevil. He would brag, and his predictions would come true. He could also flick his wrist and make the football fly seventy yards.

Another Cowboy, Roger Staubach, was the best of the 1970s. "Roger the Dodger" played on guts. He wasn't afraid of banging heads with giant linemen. He did whatever it took to win.

The 1980s had many great quarterbacks. The Dolphins' Dan Marino was a precise passer. Joe Montana—first of the 49ers and then the Chiefs—was a clutch player who always seemed to steal victories in the end. Philadelphia's Randall Cunningham was a ballet dancer among the NFL brutes.

And then there is Troy Aikman.

"He'll be the quarterback of the '90s," said Staubach. "Troy has got it all."

He sure does. Talk with men who have played with Aikman and against him and they'll tell you this: He is strong, accurate, cool. A leader. A winner.

The last word is the key. Some quarterbacks think they need to pass for 350 yards to be a star. Not Troy. He threw for 350 yards only once in his first four years in Dallas—and the Cowboys lost that game. "My goal is for the team to win," Aikman says. "It's not to make myself look good."

Many consider Troy to be the ultimate team player. No one in football prepares more for each game. No one stays up later at night, studying the game films. No one listens more closely to his coaches. No one takes more pride in victory, even if his teammates emerge as bigger stars.

He's also tougher than most fans think. Away from football, Aikman has a clean-cut, golly-gee, boy-next-door image. But other Cowboys say he can be downright tough, too. If a receiver makes a wrong turn on a pass route, Troy will get in his face. If teammates don't take a practice seriously, Troy will pick up the football and angrily punt it away. "He just wants everything to be right. To be perfect," said Cowboys guard John Gesek. "It's a matter of pride with him."

It's not surprising that when Aikman was asked after the 1993 season if he saw himself as the Quarterback of the 1990s, he shook his head no. "I've only won one Super Bowl," he said. "I've got a ways to go."

Just days after winning the 1993 championship, Troy set about trying to get back to the Super Bowl. He and the other Dallas players wanted to be a dynasty. That's a team that wins championships year after year. "I don't want to be greedy,"Aikman told reporters. "But I'd love to win two of them."

So did Cowboys owner Jerry Jones. Soon after the 1993 season started, Jones signed Aikman to a new contract. It would pay the twenty-seven-year-old quarterback $50 million over the next eight years. The deal made Troy the highest-paid player in NFL history.

Still, the season started badly for Dallas. Running back Emmitt Smith did not play in the first two games. The Cowboys lost both. Then, toward mid-season, Troy missed two games with a pulled hamstring muscle. The team lost one of those.

But when Aikman and Smith were in the lineup together, the Cowboys were nearly unbeatable—winning 11 of 12. Overall, the club went 12-4. Dallas won the NFC East title for the second straight year.

Aikman threw just 6 interceptions in the regular season, the lowest total in team history. He completed 69 percent of his passes, the fourth-best in NFL history. It was an incredible season. And teammates Smith and Michael Irvin chipped in. Together, the three stars combined for 5,916 yards and 31 touchdowns. That easily made Dallas most people's choice to return to the Super Bowl.

To get there, they had to win two playoff games. The Cowboys first faced the Green Bay Packers. The Packers were led by Reggie White, the NFL's best defensive end. Dallas won as Troy completed 75 percent of his passes for more than 300 yards.

Next, the Cowboys faced the San Francisco 49ers. It was a rematch of the previous year's NFC championship game.

The game was going great for Dallas. Troy completed 14 of 18 passes and threw touchdowns to Smith and tight end Jay Novacek. By the third quarter, the Cowboys had built a 28-7 lead and the hometown fans were cheering wildly.

Troy at the announcement of his new $50 million contract. The deal has made him the highest-paid player in NFL history.

Then, a near-disaster struck. San Francisco defensive tackle Dennis Brown accidentally banged Aikman's helmet with his right knee during a sack. Troy rose slowly, holding his helmet with both hands. When he went back to the sidelines, he seemed so confused that team doctor J.R. Zamorano decided to ask him a few questions.

"What day is it?" Zamorano asked Aikman.

"I don't know."

"Who are we playing?" Zamorano said.

"I don't know."

"Where's the Super Bowl?"

"The what?" Aikman replied.

"The Super Bowl, where you were MVP last year."

"I was?"

"Where do you play the next game?"

"Henryetta," said Troy, referring to his hometown.

With that, Aikman was taken to the hospital. The Cowboys held on to win the game. But when tests showed that Troy had a concussion, teammates and fans worried that he might miss the Super Bowl.

Troy was determined that wasn't going to happen. Despite bad headaches and dizziness, he returned to practice five days later. The Cowboys again faced the Buffalo Bills in the Super Bowl. If they could win, Troy would become the youngest quarterback in NFL history with championship rings on two fingers.

He was not to be denied. Just as they had the year before, the Cowboys stampeded the Bills. Playing before 72,817 fans at the Georgia Dome in Atlanta, Dallas won easily, scoring 30 points to Buffalo's 13.

This time, it was Emmitt Smith's turn to be a star. At the beginning of the second half, with the scored tied, 13-13, Smith carried the ball on 7 of the next 8 plays. He covered

Despite heavy blitzing from the Buffalo Bills, Troy remained calm and only released the ball when he saw an open teammate.

sixty-one yards, ending with a fifteen-yard touchdown scamper. Smith finished the game with 132 yards and 2 touchdowns on 30 carries. He was named the Most Valuable Player.

Aikman did his part, too. On the Cowboy's first play of the day, he showed that he wanted a wide-open game. Instead of running (as the Bills had expected) Aikman hit Michael Irvin on a deep slant-in for twenty yards. The play led to a field goal by Eddie Murray.

Late in the first quarter, Aikman found Alvin Harper wide-open on another deep slant route. Aikman hit Harper between the "8" and the "0" on his jersey for a twenty-four-yard gain. That set up another Dallas field goal.

Throughout the game, Troy showed his coolness under pressure. When the Bills fell behind, they began blitzing—sending five or six pass rushers at a time after Aikman. But Troy stood calmly in the pocket. He waited until the last possible instant to throw the ball. Early in the fourth quarter, for instance, the Bills sent everyone after Aikman. He beat them with a sixteen-yard strike to Harper. That took the ball to Buffalo's six-yard line. Four plays later, Smith made his second touchdown run. Dallas had clinched the game. The Cowboys became the first team since the 1989–90 San Francisco 49ers to win back-to-back Super Bowls.

In the locker-room celebration afterward, Aikman was absolutely gleeful. "It's the greatest feeling in the world," he said. "The second time feels better than the first time. And I can't wait for the third time."

The Cowboys remain one of the NFL's best teams. They still have Aikman, Smith and Irvin, plus a collection of other stars. But after their second Super Bowl win, the Cowboys went through a big change.

Aikman was all smiles as he gripped the team's Vince Lombardi trophy after Dallas won their rematch against the Buffalo Bills in Super Bowl XXVIII.

Head coach Jimmy Johnson quit the team after a public argument with owner Jerry Jones. Johnson was the brains behind the Cowboys. He was the person who put in the system that helped turn the last-place Cowboys into a winning team.

Johnson was replaced by Barry Switzer who was the coach at the University of Oklahoma when Troy went there. He is the coach who loved the offense that Troy hated so much.

As an NFL coach, Switzer did not try to change Aikman. He decided to let the Cowboys play as Coach Johnson had played them. It was good news for Troy.

Throughout the 1994 season, the Cowboys and San Francisco 49ers battled it out to see which was the best team in pro football. Aikman missed two games because of a hand injury. When he came back in a game against the 49ers, he was not sharp. He threw 3 interceptions and the Cowboys lost.

Dallas finished the season with 12 wins and just 4 losses. The Cowboys creamed the Green Bay Packers in the playoffs and then got another chance to face the 49ers in the NFC Championship game.

It was not the year for Dallas. Troy threw 3 interceptions and San Francisco won the game, 38-21. It was a disappointment for the Cowboys. But the loss made Troy and his teammates more dedicated to get back there for the next season.

"If I play twelve more years, I want to win twelve more Super Bowls," Aikman said. "Once you make the Super Bowl and win it, then I think you realize the only reason you're playing is to win the Super Bowl."

So far, so good. With the addition of superstar athlete Deion Sanders, Aikman's dedication led the Cowboys to another winning season in 1995. After breezing by the Eagles, 30–11, in the first round of the playoffs, the Cowboys battled it out with the Green Bay Packers for the NFC Championship. Aikman led the Cowboys to a 38–27 win, placing the Cowboys in the Super Bowl for the third time in four years.

Though the NFC had won every Super Bowl in the past eleven years, the Steelers proved to be a worthy opponent. Dallas took a 13–0 lead in the first quarter, but felt the Steelers closing in during the second. Neil O'Donnell threw a 6-yard touchdown pass just six seconds before the half. It looked as though the Steelers were coming back. Pittsburgh was able to close in on the Dallas lead in the second half, but O'Donnell was intercepted twice by Super Bowl MVP Larry Brown. The Cowboys held on to win as Aikman threw for 209 yards. The win made the Cowboys only the second team in NFL history to win five Super Bowls—and the first to win three Super Bowls in a four-year span.

The Cowboys finished the 1996 season 10–6, once again good enough for first in the NFC East. Dallas fought hard in the playoffs but lost to the Carolina Panthers in the second round.

In 1997, the Cowboys slipped to a 6–10 record, and missed the playoffs, but came back strong the following year. Aikman was hurt in the first game of the 1998 season, and ended up playing in only 11 games. The Cowboys, though, rebounded from the previous year, with a record of 10–6. Then, the team fell in the first round of the playoffs to the Arizona Cardinals, 20–7. Though the finish was disappointing, Dallas knows that with Aikman at quarterback there is always a chance for a return trip to the Super Bowl.

Career Statistics

YEAR	CLUB	PASS ATT.	PASS COMP.	PASS YARDS	PCT.	TD	INT.
1989	Dallas	293	155	1,749	52.9	9	18
1990	Dallas	399	226	2,579	56.6	11	18
1991	Dallas	363	237	2,754	65.3	11	10
1992	Dallas	473	302	3,445	63.8	23	14
1993	Dallas	392	271	3,100	69.1	15	6
1994	Dallas	361	233	2,676	64.5	13	12
1995	Dallas	432	280	3,304	64.8	16	7
1996	Dallas	465	296	3,126	63.7	12	13
1997	Dallas	518	292	3,283	56.4	19	12
1998	Dallas	315	187	2,330	59.4	12	5
Totals		4,011	2,479	28,346	61.8	141	115

Where to Write Troy Aikman

Mr. Troy Aikman
c/o The Dallas Cowboys
Cowboys Center
One Cowboys Parkway
Irving, TX 75063-4727

On the Internet at:

http://www.nfl.com/players/stats/career/1015.html
http://espn.go.com/nfl/profiles/profile/0615.html

Index

Miami, University of, 22, 28
Miami Dolphins, 52
Montana, Joe, 10, 52
Murray, Eddie, 58

N

Namath, Joe, 52
Nebraska, University of, 25
Neuheisel, Rick, 24
New Orleans Saints, 35, 38
New York City, 29
New York Giants, 35, 47
New York Jets, 52
New York Mets, 13, 19
Newton, Nate, 12, 41
Novacek, Jay, 12, 49, 54

O

Oklahoma, 10, 17, 19, 28, 42
Oklahoma, University of, 13, 20, 22,
    24, 28, 60
Oklahoma State University, 20, 26,
    28
Orange Bowl, 20

P

Pasadena, California, 12
Pelleur, Steve, 31
Philadelphia Eagles, 39
Phoenix Cardinals, 35
Pro Bowl, 15, 44, 46

R

Reed, Andre, 49
Rose Bowl, 12

S

San Diego Chargers, 33, 38
San Diego State, 25
San Francisco 49ers, 46-47, 52, 54,
    58, 60
Sanders, Barry, 26
Schramm, Tex, 28
Seifert, George, 46

Simmons, Clyde, 39
Smith, Emmitt, 7, 9, 38, 46, 47,
    49, 54, 56, 58
Staubach, Roger, 28, 31, 45, 52
Stepnoski, Mark, 41
Super Bowl XXVII, 7, 12, 19, 47
Super Bowl XXVIII, 56, 58

T

Texas Stadium, 28
Thomas, Thurman, 49

U

UCLA, 13, 22-26, 31, 33
Unitas, Johnny, 52

W

Walker, Herschel, 34, 38
Walker, John, 19
Walsh, Steve, 31, 35, 38
Washington Redskins, 35, 44, 47
White, Reggie, 54
Williams, Erik, 41

Y

Young, Steve, 10

Z

Zamorano, J.R., 56